I0825482

Over-the-Top Animals
Biggest Frog
By Suzane Nguyen
BLASTOFF! Beginners
BLASTOFF! BEGINNERS, AN IMPRINT OF BELLWETHER MEDIA BY FLUTTERBEE

Blastoff! Beginners are developed by literacy experts and educators to meet the needs of early readers. These engaging informational texts support young children as they begin reading about their world. Through simple language and high frequency words paired with crisp, colorful photos, Blastoff! Beginners launch young readers into the universe of independent reading.

Sight Words in This Book

a	big	help	make	they
and	can	in	the	to
are	for	it	their	use
as	from	jump	them	
away	have	long	these	

This edition first published in 2027 by Bellwether Media, Inc.

For information regarding permission, write to Bellwether Media, Inc., Attention: Permissions Department, 3500 American Blvd W, Suite 150, Bloomington, MN 55431.

Library of Congress Cataloging-in-Publication Data is available at www.loc.gov or upon request from the publisher.

ISBN: 9798893049978 (hardcover)
ISBN: 9798898801397 (ebook)

Editor: Betsy Rathburn Designer: Laura Sowers

Printed in the United States of America, North Mankato, MN.

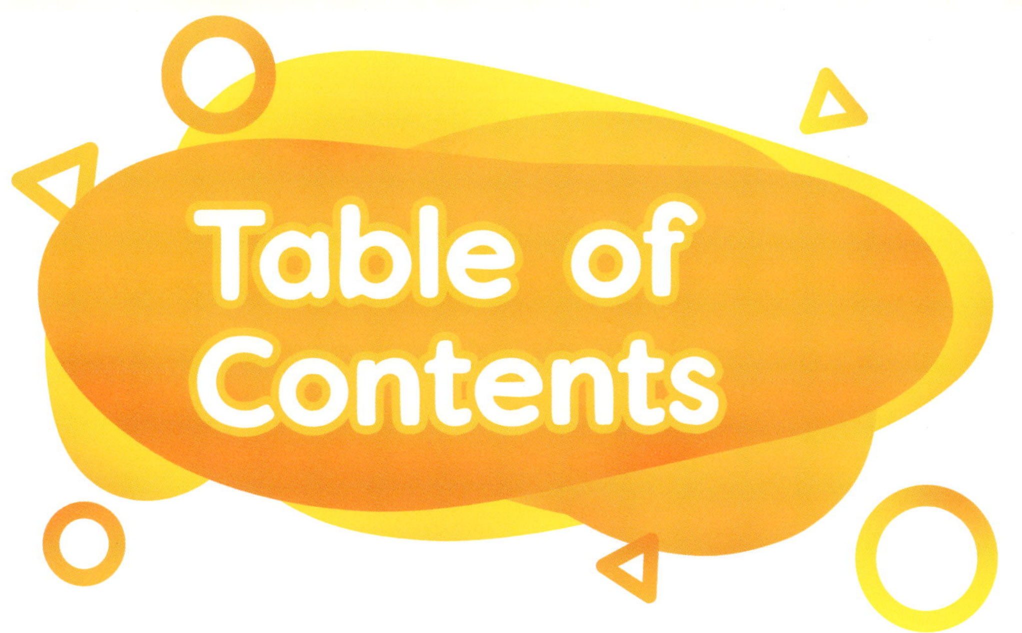

Table of Contents

A goliath frog
sits still.
It waits for food!

Hopping Hunters

Goliath frogs
are big!
They are the
biggest frogs.

They have
big bodies.
They are as big
as a cat!

They have long, sticky tongues. They pull in big **prey**.

prey

They have long legs. They can hop far!

Big Builders

These frogs are strong. They move rocks to make **nests**.

nest

Their long legs
help them.
They jump away
from danger.

They use their long tongues. They catch food from far away.

These frogs rule land and rivers!

The Biggest Frogs

Body Parts

Using Their Size

move rocks for nests

jump away from danger

catch food

Glossary

nests

places where animals rest, sleep, or have young

prey

animals that are food for other animals

To Learn More

ON THE WEB

FACTSURFER

Factsurfer.com gives you a safe, fun way to find more information.

1. Go to www.factsurfer.com.
2. Enter "biggest frog" into the search box and click .
3. Select your book cover to see a list of related content.

Index

The images in this book are reproduced through the courtesy of: Cyril Ruoso/ Minden Pictures/ SuperStock, front cover, pp. 6-7, 10-11, 14-15, 20-21, 22 (move rocks for nest), 22 (catch food); Renaud Fulconis/ Biosphoto, pp. 3, 22; Daniel Heuclin/ Biosphoto/ SuperStock, pp. 4-5, 18-19; Fabian von Poser/ imageBROKER/ SuperStock, pp. 8-9; tony mills, p. 10; Cyril Ruoso/ Nature Picture Library, pp. 12-13; Cyril Ruoso/ Biosphoto, pp. 16-17, 22 (jump away from danger); trek6500, p. 23 (nests); Allexxandar, p. 23 (prey).